GIRL POWER

INDIAN WOMEN WHO

TOOK ON THE WORLD

Published in the UK by Scholastic, 2021
Euston House, 24 Eversholt Street, London, NW1 1DB
Scholastic Ireland, 89E Lagan Road, Dublin Industrial Estate,
Glasnevin, Dublin, D11 HP5F

SCHOLASTIC and associated logos are trademarks and/or
registered trademarks of Scholastic Inc.

First published in India by Scholastic India Pvt. Ltd., 2019

Text © Neha J Hiranandani, 2019, 2021
Inside illustrations by Niloufer Wadia © Scholastic India Pvt. Ltd, 2019
Cover and pattern illustration by Aditi Kakade Beaufrand © Scholastic, 2021

The right of Neha J Hiranandani to be identified as the author of this work has
been asserted by them under the Copyright, Designs and Patents Act 1988.

ISBN 978 07023 1424 7

A CIP catalogue record for this book is available from the British Library.

Printed in the UK by Bell & Bain Ltd, Glasgow
Paper made from wood grown in sustainable forests
and other controlled sources.

1 3 5 7 9 10 8 6 4 2

www.scholastic.co.uk

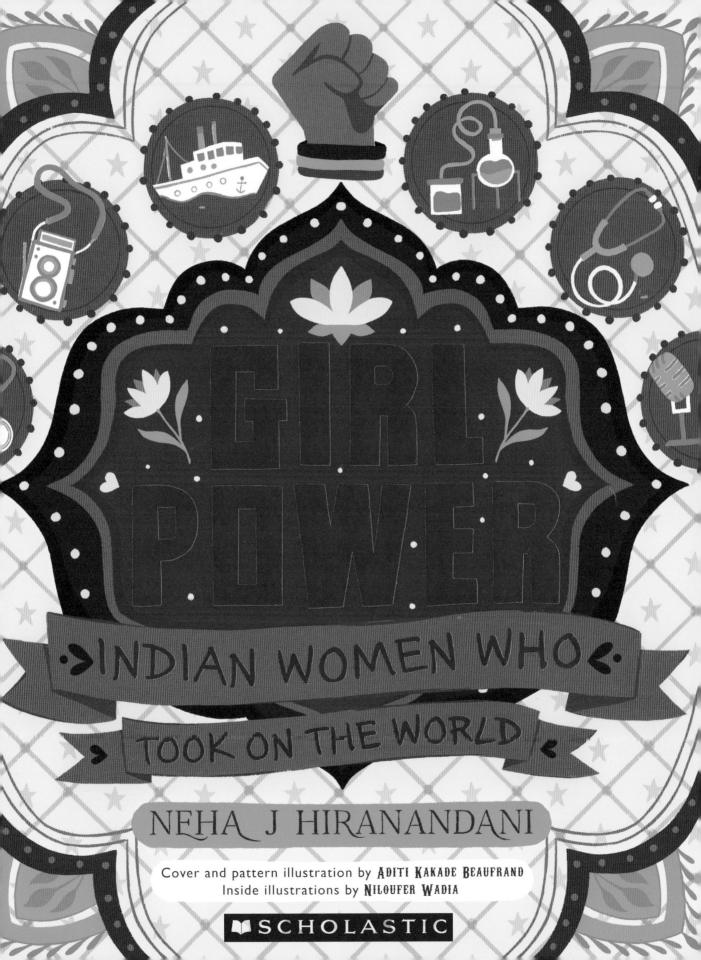

GIRL POWER

INDIAN WOMEN WHO
TOOK ON THE WORLD

NEHA J HIRANANDANI

Cover and pattern illustration by **ADITI KAKADE BEAUFRAND**
Inside illustrations by **NILOUFER WADIA**

SCHOLASTIC

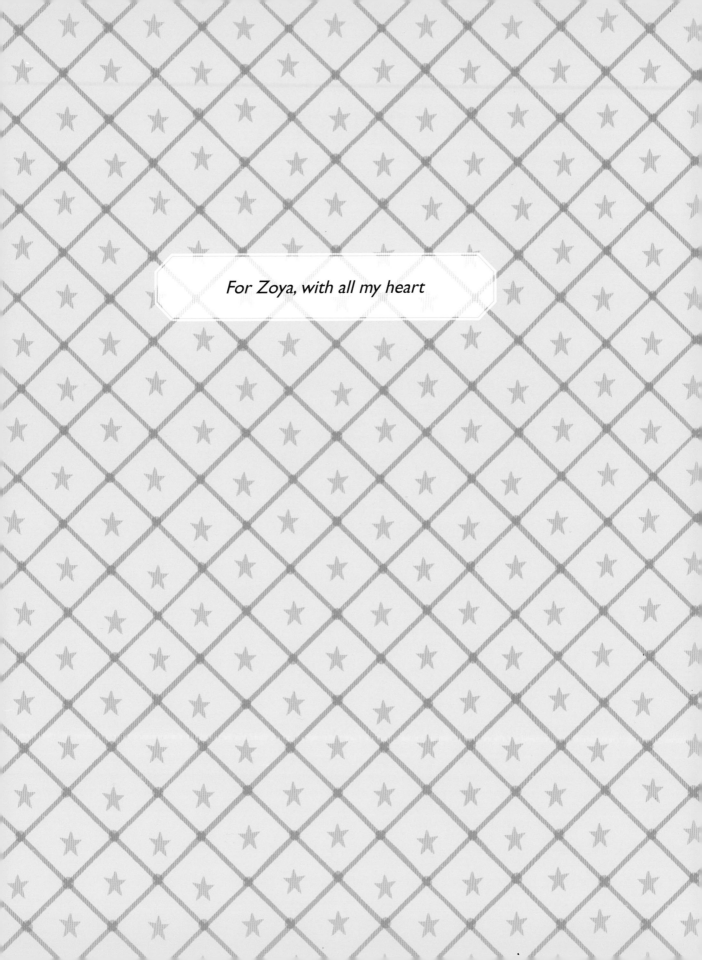

For Zoya, with all my heart

CONTENTS

ABBAKKA

WARRIOR QUEEN
(1525 – 1570)

Many years ago, close to Mangalore, stood the proud kingdom of Ullal. Rani Abbakka Chowta was its brave ruler. She was determined and fiercely independent.

Abbakka was a trained warrior and led her own army. She swore to never surrender to the Portuguese, who had been trying to capture her kingdom for many years. She even left her husband because he supported them.

Once, on a dark night, the Portuguese surrounded Ullal with their ships, ready to attack. Abbakka discovered their plot. So, she secretly gathered her best soldiers and instructed them to attack with hundreds of coconut torches and *agnivaan* – flaming arrows dipped in oil –

8

The Indian Coast Guard has named a ship, the ICGS Rani Abbakka, to honour her bravery.

all at the same time. The arrows lit up the night sky, setting the Portuguese ships ablaze before they could even touch Indian shores. The brilliant queen had saved her beloved Ullal!

Many years later, Pietro Della Valle, a famous Italian traveller, visited Abbakka. When he saw her, she was walking barefoot amongst her people, wearing a plain sari. A simple palm-leaf umbrella was held over her head. The traveller had met many great leaders, including Shah Abbas, the Persian emperor. But when the queen asked him what was there to see in the wilderness, he replied, "I came to see you, Your Majesty. You are famous."

While she was the ruler, the Portuguese attacked Ullal many times and were defeated. Abbakka was one of the strongest defenders of India, and her bravery is celebrated even today.

'[Jind Kaur] is worth more than all the soldiers of the state put together,' said Lord Dalhousie.

MAHARANI JIND KAUR

QUEEN MOTHER
(1817 – 1863)

Fearless and beautiful, Maharani Jind Kaur was an unstoppable queen. She followed her own rules and refused to veil her face. Instead, she openly ruled in court, issuing instructions to her ministers and the military.

Jind loved Punjab deeply, and did not want the British to take over her land. Since her son, Maharaja Duleep, was only five years old, she fought two wars against the British on his behalf. Unfortunately, she lost both. The British separated Jind from Duleep and she was imprisoned in Chunar Fort, in Uttar Pradesh.

It was said that whoever entered Chunar Fort never came out alive. But the brave queen vowed that she would escape the fort of death and meet her son again!

Early one morning, dressed in rags, she walked to the fort's front door. "Who are you and what are you doing here?" demanded the guard, angrily. "I'm going to the river to fetch water for the maharani's bath," replied Jind. And so, by pretending to be a maid, the clever maharani escaped the fort.

Through ferocious storms, Jind walked hungry and thirsty. With only rags to cover her, she walked hundreds of kilometres of forests, only thinking about Duleep, her beloved son. She couldn't return west to Punjab so she went north to Kathmandu. She waited there for a long time.

Then, thirteen years later, mother and son were finally allowed to meet. By then, Jind was old and almost blind but running her hands over her son's face – she knew she had finally found him.

SAVITRIBAI PHULE

TIRELESS TEACHER
(1831 – 1897)

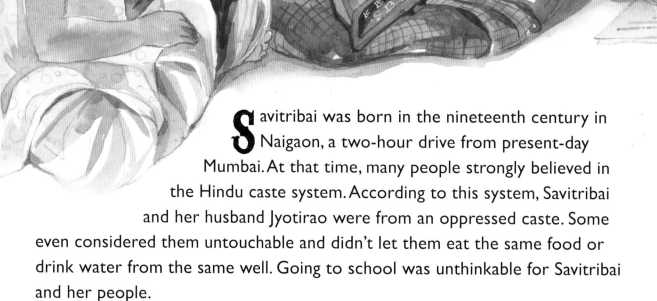

Savitribai was born in the nineteenth century in Naigaon, a two-hour drive from present-day Mumbai. At that time, many people strongly believed in the Hindu caste system. According to this system, Savitribai and her husband Jyotirao were from an oppressed caste. Some even considered them untouchable and didn't let them eat the same food or drink water from the same well. Going to school was unthinkable for Savitribai and her people.

But Savitribai was a rebel! Although she was married off at age nine, she learned to read and write and, with the help of her husband, she studied enough to become a

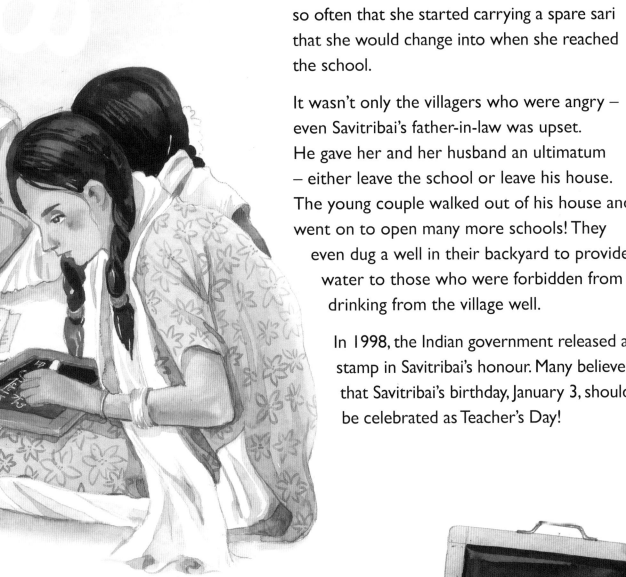

teacher. Soon after that, she and her husband decided to open a school for girls. This was revolutionary – a school for girls opened by a low-caste couple! The villagers were furious. They threw stones, mud and even cow dung at Savitribai on her way to school. This happened so often that she started carrying a spare sari that she would change into when she reached the school.

It wasn't only the villagers who were angry – even Savitribai's father-in-law was upset. He gave her and her husband an ultimatum – either leave the school or leave his house. The young couple walked out of his house and went on to open many more schools! They even dug a well in their backyard to provide water to those who were forbidden from drinking from the village well.

In 1998, the Indian government released a stamp in Savitribai's honour. Many believe that Savitribai's birthday, January 3, should be celebrated as Teacher's Day!

Savitribai was India's first female teacher.

ANANDIBAI JOSHEE

DAREDEVIL DOCTOR
(1865 – 1887)

Anandibai married very young and gave birth when she was only fourteen years old. Unfortunately, her newborn baby did not survive and Anandibai was distraught with grief. In those days, male doctors were rarely allowed to treat women and children in India. Since there were no female Indian doctors, many — like Anandibai's baby – did not get medical care and died. So, Anandibai decided to become a doctor to help the countless Indian women and children who were dying without medical treatment.

But to do so, Anandibai would have to travel to the United States of America to study medicine. No Indian woman had ever done that before. In fact, at that time, many people believed that travelling abroad was a terrible sin! But Anandibai was determined to "help the many [women] who cannot help themselves". And so, eighteen-year-old Anandibai boarded a ship to America.

Anandibai's health was poor and everything about America was different – the food, the clothes, the weather. In spite of it all, she began her studies at the Women's Medical College of Pennsylvania. She worked hard and even though she was unwell, she finished her medical degree in just two years! She was now Dr Joshee – the first female doctor of India!

Just before graduation, Anandibai received an offer to run the women's ward in an Indian hospital. She accepted the job and even dreamed of opening a medical college for Indian women. However, soon after returning to India, her health worsened and she passed away. Even though she couldn't practise medicine, Anandibai's journey was not in vain. She inspired many Indian women to break the rules and become doctors themselves.

ANANDIBAI
JOSHEE M.D.
1865 — 1887

Anandibai has
a crater on Venus
named after her.

CORNELIA SORABJI

TRAILBLAZING LAWYER
(1866 – 1954)

Born in nineteenth-century Nasik, Cornelia was the first woman to practise law, both in India and England.

Overcoming countless gender-based obstacles with determination, and her parents' support, Cornelia took admission in Bombay University and became its first woman graduate. Even though doors of lecture halls were often shut in Cornelia's face, she graduated with top marks! But Cornelia's scholarship to study abroad was denied because she was a woman. She spent the next few years arranging money herself and finally arrived at Oxford University, one of the world's top universities; Cornelia became the first woman in the world to study law there.

But even at Oxford, things weren't easy. A chaperone escorted Cornelia to lectures because all the other students were male. From her letters, it seems that Cornelia was not allowed to ask questions in class. At examination time, Cornelia faced yet another hurdle: the examiner refused to let a woman write the exams! Finally, after a special order, Cornelia was allowed to sit for the exams along with the male students.

Oxford University didn't award degrees to women at that time. So Cornelia returned to India without her degree even though she had passed the examination. She then decided to help *purdahnashins* – women who lived behind the *purdah* (curtain) and were forbidden to interact with men who weren't family. She helped hundreds of such women, and even won them the right to work as nurses.

In 1920, women started receiving degrees from Oxford, and so, about thirty years after she had graduated, Cornelia finally received her law degree!

Oxford
University
offers a
scholarship
named after
Cornelia
Sorabji.

Kamaladevi Chattopadhyay

Proud Patriot
(1903 – 1988)

When the British were ruling India, they levied a huge tax on salt. This unfair tax made salt very expensive for most Indians. Mahatma Gandhi decided that Indians would break the Salt Law by making their own salt. What an exciting moment!

Kamaladevi, a twenty-seven-year-old woman, was preparing to join the effort when she heard that Gandhi didn't want women to participate. "I was flabbergasted," she said. Kamaladevi was passionate about India's freedom – a few months ago, she had even covered the national flag with her own body when British troops

18

tried to tear it. So she rushed to meet Gandhi to convince him that women must participate in this 'great adventure'! When he eventually agreed, she was ecstatic. "I felt I had won the world," said Kamaladevi, triumphantly.

On 6 April 1930, after Gandhi made salt in Dandi, Kamaladevi marched to Mumbai's Chowpatty beach along with thousands of women. Together, they gathered sea water in their pans and boiled it to make salt. "Even as I lit my little fire to boil the sea water, I saw thousands of fires aflame, dancing in the wind," said Kamaladevi. But soon, the police charged at her and the other protestors. Kamaladevi was kicked aside and her arm fell on the burning coals. Even then she continued to guard her salt!

Kamaladevi sold this 'freedom salt' and gave the money to the freedom movement. The British arrested her for her defiance making her the first woman to be arrested in the Indian freedom struggle!

Years later, Kamaladevi was awarded the Padma Vibhushan for all that she did for her beloved country.

"We have broken the salt law, we are free. Who will buy the salt of freedom?" said Kamaladevi.

Aruna is known as the 'Grand Old Lady' of the Indian Independence movement.

ARUNA ASAF ALI

FREEDOM FIGHTER
(1909 – 1996)

During the Indian Independence Movement, freedom fighters insisted that the British leave India. As punishment for saying this, the British would often imprison them. Aruna too wanted her country to be free and was arrested several times.

In 1942, Mahatma Gandhi made a powerful speech asking the British to 'Quit India'. Gandhi announced that he along with the other leaders of the Movement would hoist the Indian flag at Gowalia Tank Maidan in Mumbai on 9 August 1942. Hoisting the flag was important – it would signal to the Indian people that the Quit India Movement had begun. But the British got wind of the plan, and they arrested Gandhi and the other leaders immediately. Now, there was no one left to lead the people! What would happen to the flag hoisting?

Aruna realized that something had to be done. The crowd was waiting and if the flag wasn't hoisted, the Quit India Movement could collapse. In front of hundreds of British soldiers, knowing that she might be arrested again, Aruna took charge. She ran towards the flag and tugging at the strings, unfurled the tricolour, signalling the beginning of the Movement. As the flag fluttered free in the breeze, the crowd cheered joyfully. In that moment, one woman had challenged the might of the entire British empire! Aruna was a heroine in the truest sense.

After India's Independence, Aruna Asaf Ali became the first Mayor of Delhi. She has been awarded the Bharat Ratna, India's highest honour in recognition of her inspiring bravery.

ISMAT CHUGHTAI

RADICAL WRITER
(1911 – 1991)

Ismat was born into a Muslim family in Uttar Pradesh, more than a hundred years ago. At that time, some Hindus and Muslims wouldn't share food because they thought they would 'pollute' one another. Sometimes, they were not even allowed in one another's houses during religious festivals.

But little Ismat was a rebel! She was good friends with Sushi, a Hindu girl. They would often take bites of the same guava even though they were from

different religions.

On Janmashtami, celebrations was being held in Sushi's house for Lord Krishna's birthday. Various snacks were being fried and Ismat was tempted 'by the appetizing aroma of the goodies'. She walked into Sushi's house – a forbidden act during the festival – and lovingly picked up the idol of baby Krishna.

What commotion followed! Sushi's family was shocked. Snatching away the idol, they threw Ismat out of the house like a 'dead lizard'. Ismat's own family was enraged. Didn't she know that Muslims didn't worship idols? But even as a child, Ismat believed that all people are made equal, regardless of their religion.

And even though she was bad at spellings, she became a groundbreaking writer!

And so, years later, when the girls met again, they continued to put aside the differences of their religions and laughingly took bites of the same laddoo!

In those days, many girls were not allowed to go to school. Ismat fought for her education, even threatening to run away and not eat food if she wasn't allowed to go to school. She convinced her parents to let her study and went on to write many powerful stories. Many of Ismat's writings focuses on the friendships between women who broke the rules. Just like Ismat's friendship with Sushi!

DAKSHAYANI VELAYUDHAN

RULE BREAKER
(1912 – 1978)

Years ago in India, there were terrible rules for a group of people called Dalits. According to the old Hindu caste system, Dalits were of a lower caste and considered untouchable. They weren't allowed to walk on the road with others, shop in the same markets or even cover their shoulders with cloth. Dalits weren't allowed into most schools and hospitals.

Although Dakshayani was Dalit, her family believed in changing these unfair rules. In fact, her mother named her after the goddess Durga, a name usually reserved for upper-caste girls.

One day, instead of covering her shoulders with beads and grass, Dakshayani wore clothes to school. School was far away, which meant Dakshayani had to take a boat and then walk for two hours. People would often throw stones at Dalits who dared to break the rules but Dakshayani persevered. She continued to wear clothes every day.

College wasn't easy either. In her science class, the upper-caste teacher refused to let Dakshayani touch the laboratory equipment. "No problem," thought Dakshayani. She learned the science experiments by watching from afar and became the first Dalit woman in India to get a college degree! Inspired by her bravery, Dalits everywhere stood up for their rights.

Wearing clothes and walking on the road with others may seem like ordinary things now, but at the time, it had taken extraordinary courage for Dakshayani to break these unfair rules. Her actions helped ensure that these unfair rules were abolished from India forever.

Dakshayani
was one of
the youngest
people to
help write the
Constitution
of India.

AMRITA SHER-GIL

REBEL PAINTER
(1913 – 1941)

As a child, Amrita had been obsessed with drawing. "I have drawn and painted, I think, from my tiniest childhood … the presents I most looked forward to as a child were paintboxes, coloured pencils, drawing paper, and picture books," she once revealed. Thanks to her European mother and Indian father, she grew up in both Europe and India. She found inspiration everywhere, from European art to ordinary Indian villagers.

After spending some time in the great art salons of Europe, Amrita grew restless. She "began to be haunted by an intense longing to return to India" and felt "there lay [her] destiny as a painter". Thus, she moved to India. "I can breathe, I can move and I can paint," she wrote, joyously. India inspired Amrita to paint some of her most famous works including *Brahmacharis, Bride's Toilet* and *South Indian Villagers Going to Market.*

Unlike most other Indian artists of the time, Amrita painted the more difficult parts of the country – the poverty of ordinary people, the heat and the dust. Her paintings were marked with such a strong connection to Indian village life, and particularly the women, that they, along with Amrita's unique artistic vision, changed the shape of Indian art forever. Perhaps she realized this when she remarked, "Europe belongs to Picasso, Matisse and Braque and many others. India belongs only to me."

Amrita's paintings are national art treasures and if you go to the National Gallery of Modern Art in New Delhi, you can find her paintings, including the priceless South Indian Trilogy.

In 1978, India Post released a stamp of Amritas painting Hill Women.

HOMAI VYARAWALLA

PASSIONATE PHOTOGRAPHER
(1913 – 2012)

Homai was studying painting while her husband-to-be, Manekshaw, was learning photography. Soon she was also drawn to the camera. As her first assignment, Homai took photos of her college friends relaxing at a picnic. These photographs were published in a magazine and everyone loved them. Homai was hooked!

In the early days, it was difficult to publish as a woman photographer. So Homai published her photos under her husband's name. Before long, she realized that she had to start out on her own. "As long as I moved around with Manekshaw, people did not take me seriously," said Homai. And so, Homai began to publish her photos under the name Dalda 13, as the license plate of her car was DLD-13! Soon enough, her work was noticed.

In 1942, Homai moved to Delhi as photographer for the British Information Service. She was India's first female photojournalist. Even though she was often dismissed as being 'just a girl', Homai didn't mind. "At school, I was the only girl [in my class]. So I was used to being in the company of boys," said Homai.

But sometimes, being a woman in a crowd of men was an advantage. When Queen Elizabeth visited India in 1961, she seemed surprised to see a woman in the crowd of male photographers. The queen turned to look at Homai and the photographer got a great shot!

Cycling through Delhi in a sari with her nine-kilo camera strapped to her back, Homai captured many iconic moments in Indian history, including the first hoisting of our flag and Mahatma Gandhi's funeral. Maybe, one of her photos is in your history book!

Homai was awarded the Padma Vibhushan in 2011.

Homai climbed to the very top of India Gate to photograph the first Republic Day Parade!

NOOR INAYAT KHAN

SPY PRINCESS
(1914 – 1944)

Noor was a princess. She was the great-great-great granddaughter of Tipu Sultan, a famous king of Mysore. She grew up in France and wrote children's stories based on the peaceful teachings of the Buddha. But Noor didn't live in peaceful times. In 1939, World War II broke out where some countries supported Britain, while others sided with Germany.

France had been captured by the enemy and Noor wanted to help Britain in the war. But, she didn't want to use any weapons. How could she help in a war without fighting? So, Noor decided to become a spy in Paris. In the middle of the night, she secretly parachuted into enemy territory. From there, she radioed enemy secrets to Britain! Her work was important and dangerous. To avoid capture, she changed her disguise every day. She moved about in secret and was very careful about who she met.

The enemy was desperate to catch the spies. They drove around with radio detection equipment in bakery vans and soon captured every spy in the network except Noor. This made Noor's already difficult assignment almost impossible. Alone in enemy territory for four months, Noor singlehandedly did the work of six people! She came up with a secret radio code and used the codename 'Madeleine', a character from her childhood stories. Even after she was captured, Noor refused to give away any secrets. She was shot, and the last word she uttered was "Liberté" meaning freedom!

Noor was awarded the George Cross, one of Britain's highest awards for bravery.

Captain Doctor Lakshmi Sahgal

Captain Courageous
(1914 – 2012)

As a young woman, Lakshmi became a doctor to serve India's poor. But as India fought for Independence, Lakshmi realized that she must first serve India as a soldier. "I had hair below my knees which my mother had never allowed me to cut. So I was really glad to have it cut and never grew it back since," said Lakshmi as she prepared for her new role as a soldier.

Lakshmi became the captain of the all-women Rani of Jhansi regiment of the Indian National Army (INA). None of the women had ever served in an army! Under Lakshmi's command, the women trained in rifle shooting, night marches and jungle warfare. In her khaki uniform, short hair and rifle slung across her shoulder, Lakshmi was a dynamic captain!

After suffering heavy losses during the war, the regiment was disbanded. Instead of going home, Lakshmi volunteered to work in an INA hospital in Burma (Myanmar). Unfortunately, the hospital was bombed and destroyed soon after. Lakshmi tried to rescue the surviving patients in bullock carts but was caught by the enemy and imprisoned for nearly two years.

Lakshmi was released in 1946 and a year later India became independent. Since she was no longer needed as a soldier, Lakshmi started work as a doctor again. For the next sixty years, she fulfilled her childhood dream of serving India's poorest patients.

A doctor and an army captain – Lakshmi proved that you can do two things in one life! For her lifelong service to India, Lakshmi was awarded the Padma Vibhushan.

Always full of energy, she ran for the post of president of India when she was nearing ninety!

M S Subbulakshmi

Raga Rockstar

(1916 – 2004)

Known as the Queen of Music, her voice ranged over three and a half octaves!

Madurai Shanmukhavadivu Subbulakshmi was born into a *devadasi* family. According to tradition, the girls from *devadasi* families were first married to temple gods, and later married and even sold to powerful men. All *devadasi* girls were expected to be adept in music and dance. Subbulakshmi's mother played the veena but try as she might, Subbulakshmi could not master the instrument.

Then her mother discovered that Subbulakshmi could easily pick up a song just by listening to it on the gramophone. Thus began her training in singing. At ten, Subbulakshmi sang in public for the first time outside a bicycle shop. Her voice was mesmerizing and people were amazed at the little girl with the incredible voice. When she was sixteen, Subbulakshmi performed at a great temple festival. The audience went wild!

Then came a problem. At nineteen, it was decided that Subbulakshmi would be married off according to *devadasi* tradition. She realized that this would mean the end of her singing career. So she took off her jewellery, quietly slipped out of the house and boarded a train to Chennai. There, with help from friends, Subbulakshmi started performing at independent concerts, breaking centuries of *devadasi* tradition! She went on to become one of the greatest talents of Carnatic music.

Subbulakshmi performed all over the world, including at the United Nations General Assembly. The former *devadasi* became the first musician to receive the Bharat Ratna award, India's highest honour. Many of her concerts were for charity as she raised money for schools and hospitals. Subbulakshmi always looked traditional with her sari and flower-adorned hair, but really she was a rebel – breaking any rules that shackled her.

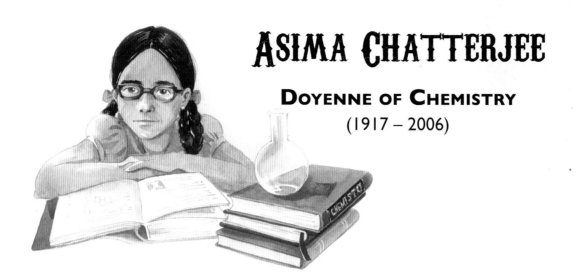

ASIMA CHATTERJEE

DOYENNE OF CHEMISTRY

(1917 – 2006)

Many years ago in Calcutta, there lived a girl named Asima who wanted to study chemistry. In those days, girls in Calcutta did not study science. But that didn't stop Asima. In fact, not only did she go on to study organic chemistry in college but she also received a Doctorate of Science – the first woman to do so in India!

Asima loved plants. She was sure that somewhere in the plants around her were the cures for many diseases. But how could she find them?

She began to study plants like Periwinkle and Marsilea Minuta (*sushni shak*). In those days, microscopes and other scientific instruments weren't easily available. So, Asima used her knowledge of chemistry and, like a good scientist, kept experimenting. After several failed experiments, her theory finally proved correct! In these plants, she found cures for diseases like malaria and epilepsy. In fact, her findings – about a group of chemicals called alkaloids – are being used in modern medicine even today.

In 1975, Asima was awarded one of India's highest honours, the Padma Bhushan.

Asima published almost 400 papers about her exciting findings!

Asima taught us that often the cures for mysterious diseases are to be found in the flora that surrounds us. Her love for plants has helped heal millions of people all over the world.

Maharani Gayatri Devi

People's Princess
(1919 – 2009)

Princess Gayatri Devi of Cooch Behar (in West Bengal) was a true princess. Her pets included exotic parrots trained to ride tiny bicycles and drive little silver cars! Gayatri had a carefree childhood – she studied in Europe, played tennis and learned horse riding. Even though she was a princess she was brought up with great freedom.

Later, Gayatri married the Maharaja of Jaipur and moved to Rajasthan. Here, life was different and very strict. The royal women observed a system called *purdah* and had to wear a veil. They could not interact freely with men – even doctors had to make their diagnosis without an examination! When Gayatri arrived in Jaipur, her car's windows were covered with thick curtains and she was asked to cover her face. This was so different from her childhood!

As the years went by, Gayatri became sure that she wanted to do away with the *purdah* for herself and others. She encouraged her husband to host receptions and invite the nobles to bring their wives. But very few came. Then she had an idea! She said to her husband, "Give me a school and I promise you within ten years, *purdah* will be broken." She wanted to educate the noblemen's daughters – the very girls who had never been to school and strictly followed *purdah*!

Gayatri succeeded in opening her school in 1943. Within a few years, the Maharani Gayatri Devi Girls' School encouraged a whole generation to come out of *purdah*.

In 1962, Maharani Gayatri Devi became the first Indian princess to stand for election where she had a fantastic victory, the biggest in the world at the time.

Maharani Gayatri Devi is admired all over the world as the princess who went from purdah to parliament.

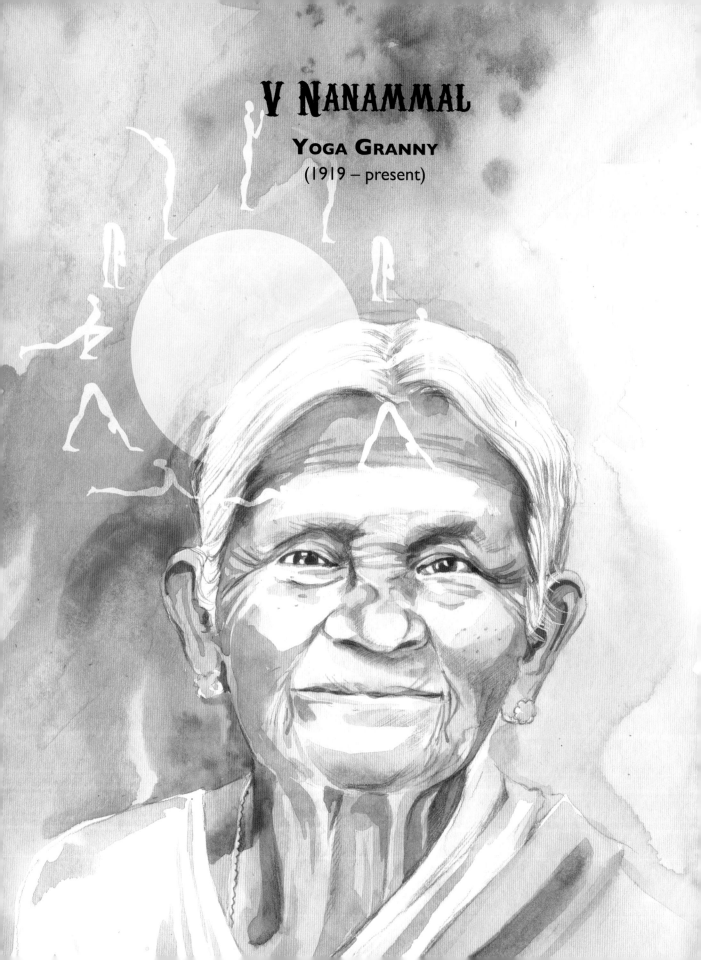

V Nanammal

Yoga Granny

(1919 – present)

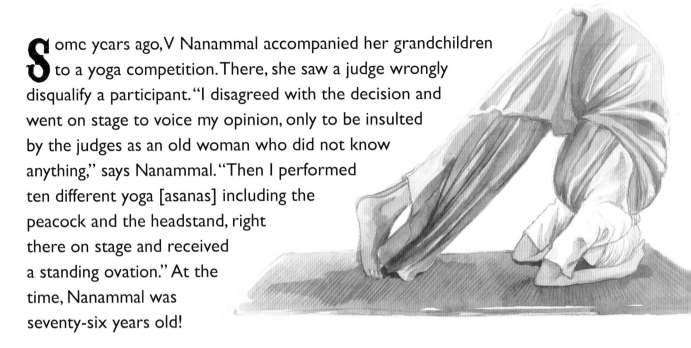

Some years ago, V Nanammal accompanied her grandchildren to a yoga competition. There, she saw a judge wrongly disqualify a participant. "I disagreed with the decision and went on stage to voice my opinion, only to be insulted by the judges as an old woman who did not know anything," says Nanammal. "Then I performed ten different yoga [asanas] including the peacock and the headstand, right there on stage and received a standing ovation." At the time, Nanammal was seventy-six years old!

Nanammal's grandparents used to work in the farms. When they returned home from work, they would practice yoga and so Nanammal started learning yoga from them when she was a young child. "These days there are gyms. In olden days, everyone did some exercise or the other. While I never formally learnt yoga, I picked it up from my grandfather just by watching him," she says.

Today, Nanammal still performs yoga every day, starting her daily practice before 5 a.m. In her whole life, Nanammal has never suffered from any serious health issues. "I have never visited a hospital in my life," she says. In fact, yoga has allowed her to heal others. "My mother-in-law was out in the farm and had sprained her leg," Nanammal remembers. "Instead of getting her to see a doctor, I offered to teach her some yoga poses and she got better." Her mother-in-law became her first student. Nanammal has taught yoga to almost a million people! She teaches over a hundred students daily and has won many awards, including the prestigious Padma Shri.

At 100 years old, Nanammal is one of the oldest yoga practitioners in the world.

USHA MEHTA

SECRET RADIO OPERATOR

(1920 – 2000)

In August 1942, Mahatma Gandhi wanted the British to 'Quit India' and needed every Indian to hear his message. But the British had put all the Indian leaders in jail. How would Gandhi get the message out?

Soon after, a young girl named Usha Mehta left her house. She had met Gandhi as a child and was deeply influenced by his teachings. And then, one day, people across the country heard her say, "This is the Congress Radio, calling on [a wavelength of] 42.34 metres from somewhere in India." Usha had started a secret radio station to help Gandhi spread his message of freedom!

The British were furious. Who was running this secret radio station? And where from? They roamed the streets in a van with radio detection equipment to hunt down the source. "The van used to chase us regularly," wrote Usha. But she and her friends kept moving their radio equipment – never using the same location twice – to avoid detection.

For three months, Usha operated the secret Congress Radio. She would broadcast news and messages about the fight for freedom, motivating thousands across India.

Towards the end of one evening's broadcast, Usha

Usha told the police to stand still while she played "Vande Mataram" on her radio!

heard loud thuds on the door. Her location had been discovered! Usha realized that she would soon be arrested. But even as the British officers broke down the door, Usha refused to interrupt her broadcast. True to form, she showed utmost bravery and dedication to her country even in the face of arrest.

For her service, Usha Mehta was awarded the prestigious Padma Vibhushan.

GAURA DEVI

PROTECTOR OF FORESTS
(1925 – 1991)

Gaura grew up in Lata, a village set amidst a beautiful forest valley in the Himalayas. One day, while collecting branches for firewood, she asked her mother why they couldn't simply cut down a big tree instead. Explaining that trees are like family, Gaura's mother said that trees hold the water from the rains and melting snow. "If anyone ever cuts down our brothers and sisters, our village will be washed away," said her mother, gently. From that day on, Gaura vowed to protect the trees that gave life to her village.

In a few years, Gaura moved to another village, Reni, which was also surrounded by a forest. One day, a young girl came running to Gaura with grave news. Lumbermen were charging towards their village; they wanted to cut down the forest to make a road.

Gaura had to do something! All the village men had already left for work. So, Gaura gathered a group of women and girls. Together, they marched to the forest and demanded that the lumbermen stop cutting the trees. The lumbermen refused. That's when Gaura knew there was only one thing left to do – she threw her arms around a tree and decided to stick (*chipko*) to it. "If you want to cut the trees down, you will have to hit us with your axes first," said Gaura. All through the cold night, Gaura and her friends hugged the trees, protecting them. The next morning, the defeated lumbermen left the village. Gaura had kept her childhood promise and saved her beloved trees!

Inspired by the *Chipko* movement (to which Gaura Devi belonged), the government banned any tree cutting in Gaura's beautiful valley.

Leila was the first woman to become chief justice of a state high court.

Leila Seth

Legal Legend
(1930 – 2017)

Twenty-four-year-old Leila was living in London with her husband and young son when she decided to study law. Although Leila worked hard, it wasn't easy to manage everything on her own. When she took the bar exam (the final law exam), Leila had two children and no help. She didn't feel prepared at all! But when the results were announced, one of her friends saw her and yelled excitedly, "Top! Top!" Leila had topped the London bar exam – the first woman to ever do so!

Armed with this victory, Leila returned to India. But in the 1950s, women lawyers were unwelcome in Indian courtrooms. "Why have you come here?" a senior lawyer asked Leila rudely. When Leila told him she wanted a job, he told her to go get married. "But sir, I am already married," replied Leila. "Then go and have a child," he said. "I have a child," she said. When the lawyer urged her to have another child, Leila replied, "I already have two children!" Amazed by her persistence, the lawyer gave her the job.

Leila proved herself by practising in courtrooms all over India, and soon became the first woman judge of the Delhi High Court. One day, she saw dozens of farmers staring at her in her courtroom. She wondered why they were there. Later, she learned that they had come to sightsee in Delhi – they had just visited the zoo and wanted to see another curious sight, a female judge! Thanks to women like Leila, female lawyers are no longer a curious sight in Indian courtrooms.

CHANDRO TOMAR

REVOLVER DADI
(1933 – 2021)

Chandro Tomar sits in her house making rotis. Later, she will milk the cows and prepare dinner. Nothing seems unusual about this grandmother … until you see her pick up a gun!

Chandro had once accompanied her granddaughter, Shefali, to the neighbourhood rifle club. Shefali was nervous, so Chandro shot a target round to encourage her. When the target paper came back, everyone was shocked. Chandro had shot a perfect ten! And so, at the age of sixty-five, Chandro started a new career.

She needed to practise keeping her arm steady. "I would fill a jug of water, and I would hold it up for an hour, lifting it the way I would lift a gun," she says. She also practiced yoga to improve her focus and threw stones at water bottles for target practice.

When others found out about her new passion, they discouraged her. Her neighbours laughed at her; saying that she was too old. But Chandro stuck to her guns. When she became the star of the Rural Olympics in 2001, Chandro had the last laugh, and soon became famous as Revolver Dadi!

Chandro is eighty-six years old now. She has fifteen grandchildren and ten times more medals! She regularly beats champions at the shooting range and provides free training to girls, many of whom have gone on to become champions themselves. Chandro says that young girls look at her and think, "If this old granny can do it, why can't we?"

By all accounts, this granny is a big shot!

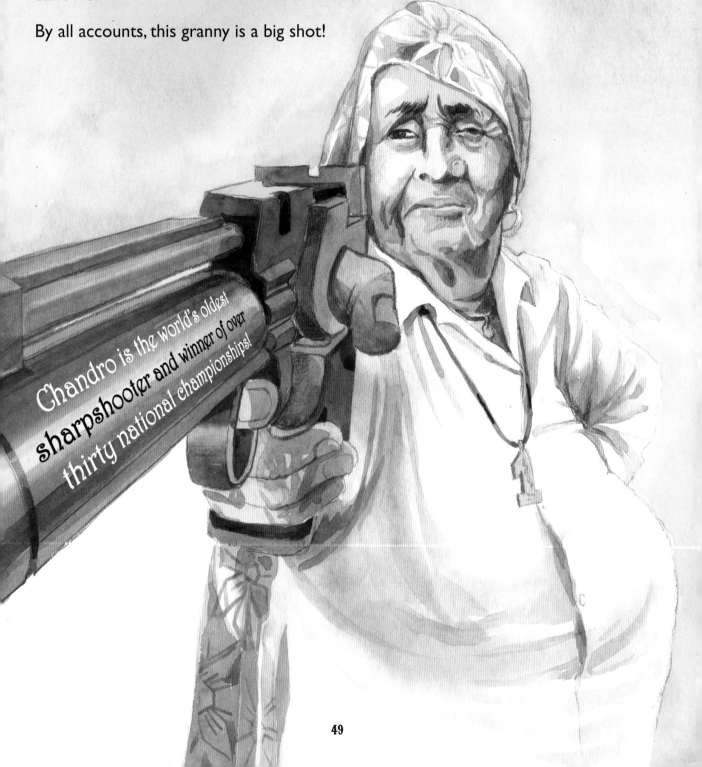

Chandro is the world's oldest sharpshooter and winner of over thirty national championships!

SHAHNAZ HUSAIN

QUEEN OF COSMETICS
(1940 – present)

Things weren't easy for Shahnaz as a teenager. "It was tough because at fourteen, I was engaged. At fifteen, I was married and had a baby," she recalls. But Shahnaz knew that she "wanted to be someone". Since she was always interested in making others look beautiful, she decided on cosmetics as a career. With her baby in tow, Shahnaz went to study cosmetics courses in London. During one of the lessons, she met a lady who had lost her eyesight because of chemically made make-up. "That's when the story of Ayurveda dawned in my mind," says Shahnaz. "If a woman can go blind with the use of make-up, there is something wrong with the beauty business."

Shahnaz started experimenting with plant cures. She would study the chemistry of cosmetic products, go back to India and try to recreate them from plants. Instead of dangerous chemicals, she created cosmetic products based on Ayurveda. Even though she had created unique products, Shahnaz didn't have the money to start a factory. She mixed her products by hand and wrote labels for each bottle herself. "I started selling from my house, making cosmetics in the kitchen," she says.

When her first herbal clinic opened in 1973, it was revolutionary. At a time when shops were selling chemical lotions to 'colour and cover', Shahnaz was providing treatments to 'care and cure'. People loved her herbal products and soon, her cosmetics business grew into a billion-dollar global conglomerate.

Shahnaz still flies all over the world to spread the message of plant healing. She was awarded the Padma Shri in 2006.

"I never rest on my laurels," says Shahnaz .

Meenakshi Gurukkal

Warrior Grandma

(1941 – present)

Like a tigress, she crouches low, muscles tight, focused on the moment. Like lightning, she slices through the air, bringing down her sword and humbling her opponent. When Meenakshi Gurukkal lands back on the ground, the crowd bows before this legendary warrior from Kerala.

Meenakshi Raghavan, respectfully called Meenakshi Gurukkal (master), has dedicated her life to *kalaripayattu*, an ancient martial art that originated in Kerala thousands of years ago. Called *kalari* for short, it is considered the 'mother of all martial arts', including karate and kung fu. *Kalari* is said to be so powerful that a master can kill someone with just a light touch!

Meenakshi started lessons when she was seven years old. Years of practice followed –

'I will teach until death,' vows Meenakshi.

flexibility training, training with wooden rods, weapons and, finally, learning to defend herself without any weapons. Kalari is not considered a woman's forte and most girls stop training in their teenage years. "There will be cuts, broken bones, bruises. That is guaranteed," says Meenakshi. But she kept training through all her injuries. Today, at seventy-seven, she is the oldest woman practising this ancient martial art!

"[My students] call me mother or grandmother," says Meenakshi. At her age, most have difficulty walking but Meenakshi wields swords and spears with ease! Many of her students, including several girls, have gone on to become masters themselves. If *kalari* is the ancient mother of martial arts, then Meenakshi is undoubtedly its modern mother.

Meenakshi was in the middle of teaching *kalari* when the news came that she was to receive the Padma Shri. Unfazed, she continued teaching until the class was over.

SUBHASINI MISTRY

DREAMER

(1947 – present)

Subhasini lived in a village in West Bengal with her husband and four children. One day, her husband fell very ill, but she did not have enough money to take him to the nearest hospital, which was in the city. Without any medical care, he passed away. That night, Subhasini vowed that no one in her village would die because of lack of money to pay for medical care. She decided to build a hospital in her village for the poor. But how? She had never been to school and couldn't count. "I didn't even know how to tell the time," she says.

For the next twenty years, Subhasini worked day and night. She cleaned ponds and collected coal from dumps; she also sold vegetables during the day and worked as a maid in the evenings. From her earnings, Subhasini saved around ₹200 every month. "I never spent anything on myself," she says. All she could think about was the hospital. Her neighbours laughed at her – they thought her dream was impossible.

But after many years, she managed to save enough to buy a tiny plot of land and build a small shed. Subhasini's hospital treated 252 patients free of cost on the very first day!

But this wasn't enough. Subhasini's dream was to build a proper hospital. So she went back to selling vegetables. Today, through Subhasini's determination, the Humanity Hospital has two floors and has treated more than 2,50,000 patients, most of them for free!

In 2018, Subhasini Mistry was awarded the Padma Shri to recognize the woman who had achieved an impossible dream.

Subhasini also
educated her son to
be a doctor and her
daughter to be
a nurse.

Tulasi Munda

Teacher Extraordinaire
(1947 – present)

Tulasi loved to learn but her parents could not afford to send her to school. When she was twelve years old, Tulasi went to live with her sister where she spent her days cutting stones and earning ₹2 per week. Even though she would be exhausted, she would return home and teach herself the alphabet.

Tulasi's people, the tribals of Odisha, were poor. She realized that the only way to end their suffering was to educate the children. So she decided to teach them herself. But the villagers weren't interested in sending their children to school. Besides, there was no school building and neither were there any teachers.

Tulasi refused to give up. She convinced the village headman to lend his verandah for a few hours. Since the children worked during the day, she decided to start a night school. She visited every house in the village and pleaded with the parents to send the children to her verandah school. Soon, the verandah filled up with thirty children.

In time, the verandah proved too small, and so Tulasi had to find a new place all over again. This time she decided to move her school under the shade of a mahua tree. To raise money to construct a school building, she sold puffed rice. This time, the villagers helped Tulasi carry stones from the mountain and build the Adivasi Vikas Samiti School. The children finally had a proper school!

As someone who didn't go to school herself, Tulasi has now educated twenty thousand children across seventeen schools.

"If you want to make a difference, you have to be selfless," says Tulasi.

BRINDA SOMAYA

AWESOME ARCHITECT

(1949 – present)

When six-year-old Brinda visited Nalanda in Bihar, she was enchanted by the ancient university. She told her mother that she wanted to be an archaeologist. Over time, Brinda's love for buildings grew and at thirteen, she decided to be an architect. Today, Brinda has designed many prestigious buildings and won several awards.

One morning, when Brinda was in Mumbai, having breakfast, she felt the floor shake. It was 26 January 2001 and a terrible earthquake shook western India. The epicentre – the point where the earthquake begins – was in Gujarat.

Brinda rushed to the state to help. She was shocked when she saw the condition of Bhadli village. It had been destroyed by the earthquake and was under a "veil of sadness". She remembers that the "people were out in the cold, their houses had been turned to rubble". The village school was destroyed too. In tears, the teachers requested Brinda to hurry and rebuild the school. If she didn't, the children would be sent to work, never to return to school again. Brinda swung into action!

She quickly created an open school while she worked on the permanent building. Over the next few months, Brinda and her team worked tirelessly, making sure to ask the villagers what types of houses they wanted and where. Then, she and her team helped the villagers rebuild Bhadli. But Brinda didn't stop there – she brought paint and mirrors so that the villagers could decorate their houses too. The once destroyed Bhadli village looked beautiful again!

Brinda says, "I am an Indian and all what I am comes from my heritage."

HALL

ROOM

GEETA SESHAMANI

BEARS' BEST FRIEND
(1950 – present)

While travelling on the Delhi-Agra highway, Geeta saw a horrifying sight – a sloth bear was being made to 'dance' for money. The bear was in pain and Geeta couldn't look away.

For centuries, sloth bears were used as 'dancing bears' in India. *Kalandars* (bear handlers) snatched cubs from their mothers when they were just a few weeks old. The helpless cubs' teeth were knocked out and their claws chopped off. Worst of all, their sensitive snouts were pierced with a thick needle and a rough rope was inserted through the wound. When the rope was pulled, the pain made the bear stand and sway, making it look like it was dancing.

Geeta realized that there were over 1200 'dancing bears' in India being dragged around miserably by their wounded noses. She teamed up with her cousin Kartick, and together, they came up with a solution: they helped the *kalandars* get other jobs and set up four rescue centres for the tortured bears. When the first bear, Rani, came to the centre, Geeta was nervous. After a lifetime of cruelty, Rani was in poor health.

But with the right care, Rani soon grew strong. Like all wild bears, she now happily forages for fruit and her favourite food – honey!

After 628 such rescues, Geeta and her team achieved an incredible milestone. In December 2009, they rescued India's last dancing bear, Raju. They had ended a cruel practice that had lasted for 400 years! To celebrate his seventh rescue anniversary, Raju was given a special 'cake' (made of watermelons) that read 'Happy Freedom Day'!

Wildlife SOS's
Agra Bear Rescue
Facility is the
largest rescue
centre for
sloth bears in
the world.

KIRAN MAZUMDAR-SHAW

ACCIDENTAL ENTREPRENEUR
(1953 – present)

Kiran's dream was to become a doctor. So, when she failed to get into medical school, she was very upset. Her father suggested that she study brewing in Australia and become a brewmaster like him, that is, someone who makes a drink called beer. She followed her father's advice. But when Kiran returned to India after her studies, she couldn't get a brewmaster's job because she was a woman. So, she

couldn't be a doctor or a brewmaster –
what could Kiran do now?

Soon after, she came across a
company that used biotechnology
to make medicines. Kiran discovered
that although she couldn't use her
brewmaster's skills to make beer, she
could use it to ferment enzymes
to make medicine! And so, Kiran
started her own company, Biocon,
in her garage. She was determined
to succeed this time. "I was willing
to do anything … when I started
my company, I didn't have money, so I
would travel all over India in a train or
on a bus. I couldn't afford a plane ticket."

Even with her determination, things
were not easy. "Banks were very fearful
of lending [money] to a woman," says
Kiran. But she continued to work hard
and made Biocon the largest company
of its kind in India. Her company makes
medicines that have helped countless
people globally. Kiran has also donated
more than $33 million, most of which
has gone towards making sure that
thousands of poor people can afford
medicines and doctors. A Padma
Bhushan and Padma Shri awardee,
Kiran is a great success!

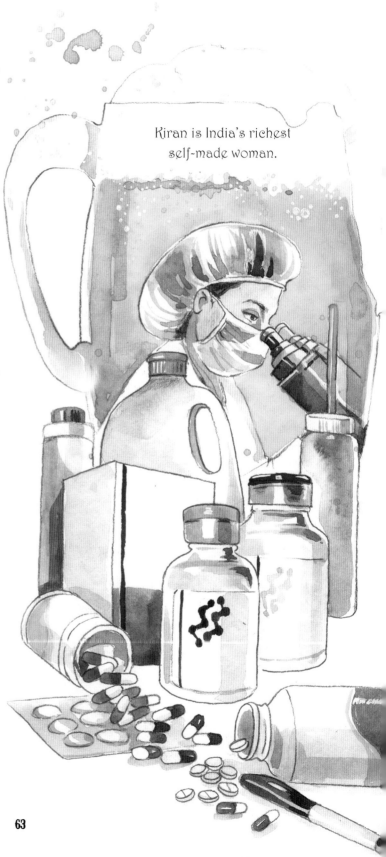

Kiran is India's richest
self-made woman.

Indra K Nooyi

Corporate Czarina

(1955 – present)

Indra's mother insisted that she get top grades. Her father and grandfather told her that if she worked hard, there was no limit to what she could achieve. They were right! After graduating from college, Indra worked twenty hours a day, seven days a week, and in 2006, she became the Chief Executive Officer (the head) of PepsiCo, a food, snack and beverage company.

When Indra joined the company, they were making products like Pepsi, Kurkure and Cheetos. These were products that Indra liked to call 'Fun for You'. But she noticed that many people now wanted to eat healthier snacks.

Indra decided that PepsiCo should create healthier snacks and introduced two new product categories: 'Better for You' and 'Good for You'. These included healthier options such as baked chips, bottled water and fruit juice. She also reduced the amount of salt and sugar in many snacks, and cut down portion sizes. Many people disagreed with her, including several of the company's employees. They demanded to know why the company needed to change when it was doing so well. But Indra was clear – she wanted to support healthier food and drinks.

And she was right. Many people all over the world loved the new products and started buying them! Under her leadership, PepsiCo became one of the most successful companies in the world.

Forbes magazine has ranked Indra as one of hundred most powerful women in the world.

Indra was awarded the prestigious *Padma Bhushan* award in 2007.

Kalpana Saroj

MAVERICK MANUFACTURER
(1961 – present)

Kalpana was born in a poor Dalit family, the lowest caste in the Hindu caste system. This meant she was always left out of sports teams in her school and never allowed to join a performance on stage. To make things worse, her family believed that girls were a burden and so, Kalpana was forced to marry at the age of twelve.

Her husband's family treated her terribly; Kalpana was regularly beaten and starved. When her father saw her six months later, he was horrified. He immediately brought her back home with him.

Kalpana got a second chance at life and decided to conquer her challenges. She learned to sew and found a job in a hosiery unit in Mumbai earning ₹2 a day. Around then, Kalpana's family lost their house and her sister fell ill. Unfortunately, ₹2 a day wasn't enough to save her sister's life. "[That was the moment] I realized I had to make money," says Kalpana.

So she decided to become an entrepreneur. She borrowed money from the government and started a business. Soon after, she came across a factory that was shutting down but could be saved if it had a strong leader.

Kalpana thought about the poor factory workers and decided to take a chance. Under her leadership, the company was transformed and, the girl who once earned ₹2 a day created a business worth millions!

In 2013, Kalpana was awarded the Padma Shri, one of India's highest honours.

'Hard work is not overrated. It is fail proof,' says Kalpana.

KALPANA CHAWLA

AMAZING ASTRONAUT
(1962 – 2003)

Once, there was a girl in Haryana who didn't have a name. Her parents nicknamed her Montu, but her teacher said she needed a real one. The little girl said, "I will be Kalpana" – choosing a name which means imagination. Soon, the little girl with the big imagination began to think about space. She loved looking at the stars and drawing aeroplanes.

Once during a mathematics class in school, Kalpana's teacher was explaining null sets or empty sets. "A set of Indian women astronauts is a null set as there are none," said the teacher, as an example. Kalpana replied, "But ma'am, one day this set may not be empty!"

Kalpana made sure to fill the empty set. When she was just twenty-six years old, she joined NASA, the American agency that conducts space research. Before long, she became the first Indian woman to travel to space! She was selected for exciting missions where she rocketed out of Earth and worked the robotic arms of a spaceship.

While on board Space Shuttle Columbia, Kalpana spoke to I K Gujral, the then Indian prime minister. "The view of the Himalayas is magnificent!" she exclaimed, looking at India from space. She promised him that she would visit India when she returned to Earth. Unfortunately, minutes before the shuttle was supposed to land on our planet, an accident occurred killing everyone on board.

From the girl without a name, Kalpana went on to have many things named after her – streets, asteroids and supercomputers.

MEGHA GOKHALE

PATH-BREAKING PRIEST
(1962 – present)

Priests are important to Hinduism and it isn't easy to become one. Historically, the training often begins at a young age with a focus on learning sacred texts, mantras and Sanskrit. Priests follow a strict lifestyle, both physically and mentally, so that they can perform temple prayers and sacred ceremonies.

For centuries, temples and religious ceremonies have been dominated by men, even though Hindu scriptures don't forbid women from becoming priests. But some women like Megha Gokhale are challenging the norm!

Megha was a little girl when she was introduced to Hinduism by her grandfather. "Like a sponge, I would absorb everything my grandfather taught me," she remembers. His teaching sparked her interest and soon young Megha was studying the *Bhagavad Gita*. She even memorised the difficult *shlokas* in the ancient scriptures.

India has around 1600 female Hindu priests now.

Years later, Megha decided to attend a priest school for women, where she recited 'paths' (religious incantations), studied Sanskrit and learned how to perform rituals and ceremonies. Armed with this knowledge, she became one of the few female priests in India!

Things weren't easy in the beginning and she was often rejected in favour of a male priest. But she persevered and today, twenty-three years after she began her journey as a priest, many families want her – a woman – to perform pujas for them.

Megha's life as a priest includes waking up before sunrise, performing ceremonies and even training other men and women who want to be priests.

It is hard work breaking the rules but Megha enjoys doing it!

Bula Chowdhury

Ace Swimmer
(1970 – present)

One day, Bula's father was travelling in a boat. Suddenly, it started to sink and he didn't know how to swim! Luckily, a swimmer saved him from drowning. That's when he decided that his children would be swimmers. And thus, when she was just two years old, Bula learnt to swim in the pond outside her house. She took to the water like a fish. Soon, she started training at a club and won her first national swimming competition at the age of nine.

Growing up, Bula dreamed of swimming in the open sea. Unfortunately, she was diagnosed with a severe seawater allergy. "My skin would burn and itch all night after the swim. But I wasn't going to let such obstacles stop me from pursuing my dream," says Bula.

In 1989, Bula decided to conquer the 'Everest of Swimming' – the English Channel. And that meant swimming from England to France! Swimming across the channel was not easy. It required continuous swimming in freezing

water, for hours on end. She would have to navigate around massive ships and even jellyfish! "The water was so cold that when I put my foot in it, I thought this is impossible," says Bula. After swimming for a while, she was exhausted, and when she looked up from the water, she couldn't see the shore. But failure was not an option. Bula didn't stop. After swimming for ten hours and forty-six minutes, Bula crossed the channel!

An Arjuna Award and Padma Shri recipient, Bula says, "I should have been a fish," as she thinks of her swims.

Bula is the first woman in the world to swim across the seas of five continents.

Radhika is the first female captain in the Indian Merchant Navy.

Captain Radhika Menon

Super Sailor
(1974 – present)

In June 2015, seven fishermen went fishing in a small boat named the *Durgamma*. They did not know that a terrible storm was brewing. Soon, their boat was being tossed about by tempestuous winds and twenty-five-foot-tall waves! The engine had failed, the anchor was lost and the food washed away – how would the fishermen survive?

Meanwhile, caught in the same storm was a ship headed by Captain Radhika Menon. "We were also having a very tough time," remembers Radhika. "Our ship was … in a very bad condition."

In the middle of battling the storm, Radhika's team noticed a black spot amongst the massive waves – it was the *Durgamma* with the fishermen huddled inside! Radhika immediately ordered a rescue operation.

As the winds raged, the *Durgamma* was swept away in the direction opposite to Radhika's ship. Somehow, Radhika's team dropped a rescue rope and managed to bring two fishermen to safety. Then, suddenly, the rescue rope snapped in the fierce weather – the *Durgamma* was being taken by the storm again!

Radhika didn't give up. Battling waves as tall as a building, she kept making rescue attempts until all seven fishermen were brought to safety! "Madam appeared [like] a goddess and saved our lives," a survivor remembers.

Although bravery is just part of the job for her, Radhika became the first woman seafarer in the world to receive the International Maritime Organization Award for Exceptional Bravery at Sea! "As a seafarer and Master [of my ship], I have just done my duty," says Radhika humbly.

Chhavi Rajawat

Savvy Sarpanch

(1977 – present)

Deep in Rajasthan is a village named Soda that had very little water. There were no proper roads and hardly any toilets. "I didn't know where to begin," says Chhavi, the sarpanch (village head) of Soda.

Chhavi Rajawat isn't your average village girl – she wears jeans and sunglasses, speaks English and has worked in big cities. "I know I don't fit the typical mould of a sarpanch," she says. But Chhavi's family is from Soda and she loved spending her school vacations there. When the condition of the village worsened, Chhavi decided to help. "I am the daughter of the village," she says proudly, "and if I don't help then how can I expect an outsider to help?" Leaving her big-city job, Chhavi plunged into village life.

Soda's biggest issue was water. Chhavi saw that the village reservoir – a large pond – could collect rainwater, but it hadn't been cleaned in more than seventy-five years! Chhavi was determined to clean the reservoir before monsoon began. In just four days, Chhavi single-handedly raised money to clean the reservoir. Soda would now have enough water to drink!

Chhavi didn't stop there. She also made sure that the houses in the village had electricity and toilets. Although Chhavi built many new roads in Soda, her own path was difficult. Some mischievous people, who didn't want her in the village, attacked her with sticks and stones. But Chhavi hasn't given up. "I'll surely make this a model village," she says about Soda.

As a child, the village elders carried Chhavi on their shoulders, and now she carries the entire village.

ग्राम पंचायत सोडा
पंचायत समिति मालपुरा जिला - टोंक (राज.)

Chhavi is one of the youngest sarpanches in India.

HARSHINI KANHEKAR

FEARLESS FIREFIGHTER
(1979 – present)

Growing up, Harshini was a part of the National Cadet Corps where she noticed how officers wore their uniforms with pride. She too dreamed of being a uniformed officer one day. Soon, she came to know about the National Fire Service College that trained firefighters and they wore uniforms! But, there was a catch – the college had never had a female student!

When Harshini walked into the college for admissions in 2002, everyone looked at her suspiciously – what was a girl doing there? But Harshini cleared the admission process and became the first girl to be admitted to the college. She was ecstatic.

Still, many people mocked her choice of career, and she began to feel the weight

FIRE SERVICE

of her position. She realized that she was representing girls everywhere! "If I came late, people would say that girls come late. If I fail to lift equipment, people would say that girls are weak." So Harshini made sure she reached college early every day. "I would [even] practise lifting equipment in the storeroom so that I [wouldn't] fail in front of people," she says.

After graduating, in 2005, she received an alarming phone call: a shoe factory was burning and the building was falling apart. Harshini and her team climbed the opposite building and tried dousing the fire, but it didn't work. The smoke kept rising. There was no choice — risking their lives, they climbed the crumbling building. After a six-hour-long operation, Harshini and her team successfully controlled the fire!

"No field of work belongs to any gender," says Harshini as she dons her beloved uniform.

Harshini is India's first female firefighter.

MANJU DEVI

COOLEST OF COOLIES

(1980 – present)

Manju's husband worked as a coolie in Jaipur Railway Station. After he passed away, the family were left penniless. "We didn't have water to drink. And no food to eat," says Manju. When she looked at her three hungry children, Manju knew she had to do something. She decided to become a coolie and applied for her husband's old job. Everyone was shocked. "But why can't women be coolies?" asks Manju. "Women till the fields, we work with buffaloes. We can do difficult work too."

And so Manju began work at Jaipur Railway Station. In the beginning, Manju was confused. She couldn't tell the station platforms apart. "Where would the train from Mumbai arrive? And the train from Chennai?" Manju wondered. She couldn't read and all the signs looked the same to her. But with time and training, Manju learned. Today, she can easily load bags on and off the train as well as carry several kilos of luggage on her head!

Since the railways had never employed a female coolie before, they didn't have a uniform for Manju. So, she designed one herself and wears her red-and-black salwar kameez with pride. Manju wishes more women would do the kind of work she does. "If more women could carry heavy burdens, then we would be seen as equal to men," she says.

Manju has sent all her children to school with her earnings. She was recently honoured by the president of India who was deeply moved after hearing Manju's incredible story.

MISS WORLD · 2000 ·

Priyanka Chopra

Superstar

(1982 – present)

Priyanka Chopra is one of India's most famous actors. As a teenager, she went to study in the USA. She was the only Indian in her school and because of this a group of girls constantly bullied her. "They would push me against the wall and call me 'brownie'," remembers Priyanka. "I'd walk by and they'd say, 'Can you smell the curry?'" The bullying scared her. "I started believing that I was less," she says. For years, she didn't enter the school cafeteria and would instead buy a bag of chips from the vending machine and eat her lunch in the storage room.

One day, Priyanka realized that it was the attitude of the people that needed to change and not the colour of her skin! She got over her fears and made her vulnerability her strength. She moved back to India, won beauty pageants and pursued a career in acting. It wasn't an easy path but she refused to give up. "I don't want any kid to feel the way I felt in school," she says. Motivated by her experience, Priyanka went from being an insecure teenager to a global movie star. She says she got here by following the three Fs—"by being fierce, by being fearless and by being flawed".

After a successful film career in India, Priyanka moved to Hollywood, USA. This time no one dared to bully her. In 2016, Priyanka became the first Indian to win a People's Choice Award.

Priyanka won the Miss World pageant in 2000, when she was only seventeen years old!

MARY KOM

LEGENDARY BOXER

(1983 – present)

Surrounded by rice fields in Manipur, Mary Kom worked in a farm as a child. She loved sports but her parents had no money to support her passion.

As a teenager, Mary moved to Imphal, the capital of Manipur. While she was there, she heard about a Manipuri boxer, Dingko Singh, who had just won a major championship. Dingko was poor like her. "If he can do it, so can I," thought

Mary, inspired. She went to a boxing coach and asked for training. The coach laughed, saying, "No! You are a girl and too small and thin." But Mary convinced the coach and began boxing every day, often sparring with her own reflection in the mirror.

Back home, Mary's father did not want her to box as he thought that it would ruin her face and chance of getting married. One morning, her father saw a newspaper article about a young boxing champion. The photo was blurry. Who was it? He wondered.

Mary is a five-time World Boxing Champion and Olympic medalist.

Before her father could find out, Mary came home clutching a gold medal! This was the first of many medals. Her passion won her parents' support and everyone began calling her 'Magnificent Mary'. She says, "Each medal I have won is a story of a struggle."

Mary now has three children and continues to box. "When I started, they said boxing is not for girls. But I want to show that I can make history for India," she says.

Mary is amongst the lightest of championship boxers. Though she is small, she is mighty.

'In five years, if everyone is not motivated to manage their own garbage, I will still consistently be doing the same thing,' says Temsutula

TEMSUTULA IMSONG

CLEANLINESS CRUSADER

(1983 – present)

When Temsutula arrived in Varanasi, she was shocked! One of the world's most sacred cities was also one of the dirtiest. Varanasi has many steps, called *ghats*, leading down to the river Ganga.

When Temsutula first saw Prabhu Ghat, it was covered with garbage. People were even using it as a bathroom! "We had to hold our breath," remembers Temsutula. "There was garbage and excrement everywhere. There was no place to even stand." Temsutula was very upset. How could the people of Varanasi be so disrespectful towards their own heritage?

Temsutula decided to clean the ghats herself. But how? She was from Nagaland and she didn't know anyone in Varanasi. Using the hashtag #MissionPrabhughat on social media, she inspired others to join her. A month later, Temsutula returned with a small team. Armed with brooms and gloves, they set to work. On the first day, they covered Prabhu Ghat with bleach. Then, over three days, they transported more than three hundred kilograms of garbage to the dumping grounds. On the last day, Temsutula tweeted a photo – the ghat was spotless!

Temsutula's work is difficult. It takes days to wash the smell from her body. She spends weeks cleaning a ghat only to see it dirtied in minutes. But Temsutula refuses to give up. She has asked Varanasi's schoolchildren to join her and to tell their parents to stop littering. She hopes that people will soon learn to recycle their waste and manage their own garbage.

Temsutula can usually be found on Varanasi's ghats with a broom in her hand, cleaning and promoting cleanliness.

Pabiben Rabari

Digital Designer
(1984 – present)

"Overcoming hurdles, that's been my passion since childhood," says Pabiben.

Pabiben grew up in Bhadroi village in the desert region of Gujarat. After her father's death, her mother was left alone to raise three children. Pabiben helped her mother by drawing water from wells for a rupee. She stopped going to school after class four and took up thread-and-mirror embroidery – something that her tribe, the Dhebaria Rabaris, is known for.

Soon, she was making beautiful designs for bags, carpets and other items. She even created her own style of machine embroidery using trims and ribbons.

One day, her husband said to her, "Why don't you start your own company?" And so she did! In 2015, Pabiben asked a few village women to join her. Believing that people need not leave the village to earn a living, she asked them to work from home.

Pabiben's sample bag – the 'Pabi Bag' – was a big hit at the first sale exhibition she attended. She was on the right track but now she had to figure out how to grow her business. That's when she decided to go digital with a website in her name! "I am not an educated person, so it took longer for me to put my business online," says Pabiben. Going online in a desert village like hers was revolutionary. But she says, "People do new things from the city. I wanted to do new things from the village." So, she transformed herself into pabiben.com!

Today, Pabiben's monthly income has increased more than a hundredfold. She employs around sixty women. Her husband has left his job to join her team. From her village, Pabiben supplies embroidered items all over the world and her bags have even been featured in Bollywood and Hollywood movies!

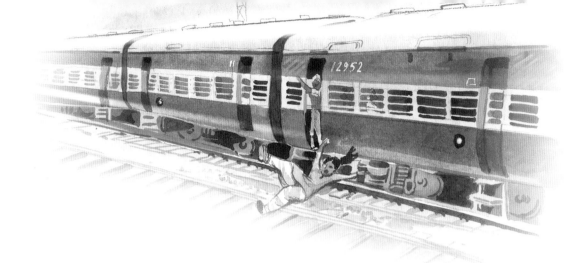

ARUNIMA SINHA

FORCE OF NATURE
(1988 – present)

Arunima was a national-level volleyball player. When she was twenty-three years old, she was attacked by robbers on a train. Arunima tried to fight them off but they threw her out of the coach. She suffered terrible injuries and her left leg had to be amputated. It was an awful thing to happen, especially to someone who loved sports.

But Arunima refused to give up on life. While still in the hospital, she asked herself, "What would be the most difficult thing to do right now?" And that's when she had an idea! She would climb Mount Everest, the world's highest mountain, with one artificial leg and a metal rod in the other!

After a year of training, Arunima faced the mountain. The climb was doubly difficult for her. Her artificial leg slipped on the ice several times, and the strain made her leg bleed. "Many times, the prosthetic leg just came off on the mountain and I fell," remembers Arunima. But with her eye on the summit, she kept going. When she was just a few hours away from the peak, she realized that her oxygen cylinder was running out! "Go back!" insisted the team leader but Arunima refused. "I had to hoist the Indian flag on the top," she says. After climbing for fifty-two days, she finally reached the peak. Arunima hoisted the Indian flag in the snow and became the first female amputee in the world to climb Mount Everest!

Within two years of losing her leg, Arunima had climbed to the top of the world! She is the epitome of courage and spirit.

Arunima has since climbed six of the world's seven highest peaks.

Malvika believes her disability is her superpower!

MALVIKA IYER

BRAVEHEART
(1989 – present)

Malvika was only thirteen years old when a tragic accident changed her life forever. She had been mending her torn jeans and was looking for something that could put pressure on the fabric. She found a blunt object in her garage that she thought she could use. Little did she know that it was a bomb. It had landed in her garage when the nearby ammunition depot had caught fire some time back.

The bomb exploded.

Malvika lost both her hands. Her legs were so damaged that she was unable to walk. For eighteen months, Malvika experienced unimaginable pain as doctors performed several surgeries on her.

Soon, the tenth class board examination loomed. Malvika was in a wheelchair with no hands. She realized that she had two choices: surrender to her wounds and give up, or fight and win! Malvika decided to fight. With only three months left, she began her exam preparations. Learning calculus, biology, physics – there was so much to be done in such little time! Malvika attended the examinations in crutches and a scribe wrote the answers for her. The results changed her life forever. Malvika was a state topper who had scored hundred per cent marks in both maths and science!

Today, Malvika has a doctorate in social work and is a motivational speaker. She has even spoken at a United Nations forum and received a standing ovation. The president of India recently awarded her the Nari Shakti Puruskar, India's highest civilian award for women. In many of her speeches, you can hear Malvika saying, "The only disability in life is a bad attitude. Going by this, I don't think I have a disability!"

LAXMI

FASHION PHOENIX
(1990 – present)

Laxmi was a beautiful fifteen-year-old girl who dreamed of being a singer. Unfortunately, an older man kept harassing her, asking her to marry him. When she refused, he decided to take revenge. One day, in 2005, while she was walking down the street, this man and his accomplice followed her and threw acid on her face. "It felt like my whole body was on fire," Laxmi remembers. "My face was melting like plastic." She was rushed to the hospital where doctors worked hard to save her life.

When Laxmi finally looked in a mirror, she was shocked by her disfigured face. "I had no nose, the lips were somewhere, the ears were somewhere else … my face was completely ruined," she says. Her father comforted her and said that one day she would find her face beautiful again. "Nothing is impossible," said her father, gently.

Laxmi's father was right. Over time, she started loving her face. She began designing and tailoring beautiful clothes that she wore with pride. Her family was her biggest support and with their help, she began to dream again. Laxmi wishes she had told her parents about the man before the attack. "I can't stress enough on how important that is," she says.

Today, Laxmi has walked the ramp for a fashion show in

Laxmi has successfully campaigned to restrict the sale of acid in India.

London and modelled for a fashion brand. She has proved to the world that she is not going to lose her courage.

"He threw acid on my face, not on my dreams," Laxmi says with a beautiful smile.

SAKSHI MALIK

CHAMPION WRESTLER

(1992 – present)

Sakshi was twelve years old when she first tried wrestling. "It called out to me," she says. "I felt like it was made for me." Sakshi lives in Haryana where girls often can't even leave the house, much less become wrestlers. Many people were surprised and said things like "why does a girl want to be a wrestler?" and "she'll stop looking like a girl". But Sakshi didn't pay attention to these comments and, luckily, her family supported her decision to wrestle.

It wasn't easy as Sakshi had a gruelling schedule. "The school bus would come at 6.30 a.m. I would get up at 4 a.m., train for a bit, attend school, return, go for my tuitions and then train again," remembers Sakshi.

Her training room didn't have fans or lights, but it did have posters of well-known wrestlers on the walls. Sakshi would dream of the day when posters of her would hang there too.

Determined and focused, Sakshi trained for twelve years and qualified for the 2016 Rio Olympics. In her final match, she was down by 0 – 4 points and winning seemed impossible. But Sakshi had predicted that she would win an Olympic medal. And sure enough, with just seconds remaining, Sakshi attacked her opponent and won the match! "Those ten seconds changed my life," she declares.

Sakshi became the first Indian to win a medal in the 2016 Rio Olympics. Her victory made a billion hearts smile. Sakshi has also been awarded the Khel Ratna, India's highest sporting honour.

"The medal will be mine!" says Sakshi.

DIPA KARMAKAR

EXTRAORDINARY GYMNAST

(1993 – present)

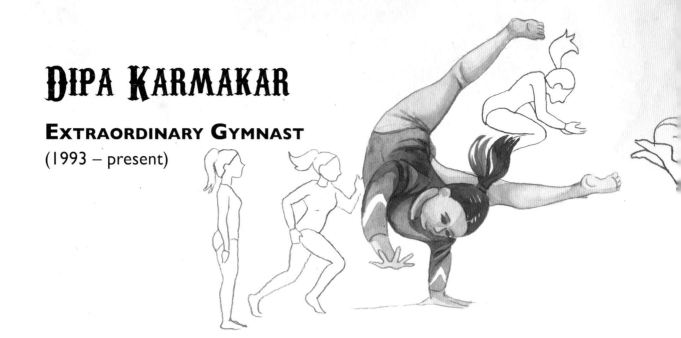

When she was five years old, Dipa's gymnastics coach promised her a Big Babol chewing gum, if she could mount the uneven bars. Using all the strength in her body, little Dipa climbed the bars and got the gum! Each gum came with a sticker and Dipa was doing so well that soon her entire cupboard was covered in stickers!

Dipa was flying from challenge to challenge, but then came devastating news. She was flatfooted which made the already difficult vaults almost impossible. Was this the end of her dream?

Her coach gave her foot exercises to do daily, and she exercised her feet before and after practice. Within a year, her feet developed a natural curve and Dipa was on her way to becoming a national champion!

Even then, people would jeer saying nasty things like "she is a buffalo and her coach is a donkey" and "India's women gymnasts [are] good for nothing". But Dipa didn't give up. She became the first Indian woman gymnast to qualify for the Olympic Games. At the 2016 Olympics, Dipa soared through the air becoming one of the few women in the world to perform the Produnova vault, often called the 'vault of death'!

After her stunning Olympics performance, Dipa was awarded the Padma Shri. She was thrilled and wanted her coach to receive the award with her. And so,

Dipa is the first Indian woman gymnast to qualify for the Olympics.

at the award ceremony, she wore her coach's white socks underneath her sari so that he could be a part of her hard-won victory!

DEEPIKA KUMARI

INSPIRATIONAL ARCHER
(1994 – present)

Deepika was born by the roadside, in a place close to Ratu village in Jharkhand, one of the poorest parts of India. Growing up, there was no fan or bathroom in her house and the only furniture was a single bed which the family shared. Although her parents worked hard, often there wasn't enough money for meals, let alone fruits. Luckily, the mango trees in the neighbourhood bore fruit and Deepika would aim at those with stones. Soon, Deepika was able to shoot them down with a homemade bamboo bow and arrow!

Around the time, Deepika heard about an archery academy where archers were trained for free. She was shocked! For her archery had meant hitting mangoes with homemade arrows – could it be a real sport?

When she arrived at the academy, however, the coach was sceptical – Deepika looked so weak! "Give me three months," she said. "If I'm not good enough, you can kick me out of the academy." But, soon the academy became her new home and archery her life.

The villagers of Ratu thought that Deepika should "stay at home [rather] than compete in the

Deepika became world number one in archery at the age of eighteen!

Olympics in short pants." But like a true archer, Deepika did not get distracted and stayed focused on the bullseye!

Within a few years, Deepika became the best archer in the world in her category! She was honoured with the Arjuna Award and the Padma Shri.

Today, in place of her family's hut, Deepika has built a much bigger house for her parents.

"I want my story to inspire every girl," says Deepika.

P V SINDHU

STAR SHUTTLER
(1995 – present)

indhu's parents were volleyball players but as a little girl, she fell in love with badminton. Inspired by P Gopichand – who became her coach – Sindhu would travel fifty-six kilometres every day to train with him. She was just eight years old.

Today, P V Sindhu is always on the badminton court. "I have never taken a vacation," she says, smilingly.

Every day, Sindhu reaches the court by 4.30 a.m. She trains for the next seven hours with just two small breaks.

Once, while training, Sindhu fractured her leg and it had to be put in a cast. It was a painful injury and any other person would have rested, but not Sindhu! With a cast on one leg, she spent her time training the rest of her body.

During the year before the 2016 Olympics, Sindhu increased her training time. She stopped eating all her favourite foods, especially ice cream, and even gave up her phone.

At the Olympics, Sindhu's hard work paid off and she reached the finals where she had to play against Marin, the world's top badminton player. She tried her best, but Marin won. And then, something amazing happened … everyone turned to look at Sindhu! Because even though she had just lost the gold, she did not lose her cool. She walked over to Marin, hugged her, picked up her fallen racquet and placed it on her bag. Her respect for the game made her a winner in the eyes of the world!

Sindhu was awarded the silver medal at the 2016 Olympic Games. Then she finally had some ice cream!

P V Sindhu is the youngest Indian to win an Olympic medal.

Poorna Malavath

Everest Conqueror
(2000 – present)

Poorna grew up in a small tribal village in Telangana where the land is as flat as a sheet of paper. One summer, she went for a rock-climbing camp far away from her village. Looking up at the steep Bhongir Rock – the rock she was supposed to climb – Poorna was scared. But she decided to give it a shot and by the time she reached the top, all her fears had disappeared. The coach asked her what she knew about mountaineering and Mount Everest, to which she truthfully replied, "I am

At thirteen, Poorna is the youngest girl in the world to climb Mount Everest.

hearing about it for the first time."

Just months after that conversation, Poorna was standing below Mount Everest, looking up at its snowy peak. She had spent eight difficult months in training, determined to prove that 'girls can do anything' including climb Earth's highest mountain! That day a fierce storm was raging on Everest and many experienced mountaineers had died trying to climb the mountain. Poorna's mentor told her to come back, but she said that she didn't have a reverse gear. She was determined to keep moving forward.

It took Poorna fifty-two days to climb Everest. On the morning of 25 May 2014, the final day, Poorna saw her first dead body — a mountaineer who had died trying to do what she was attemtping. She says, "Just before that, I had suffered dizziness because my oxygen had run out. I wanted to sit, but there was no place; the only way was up. The sight of the dead body made me shiver, and for the first time I thought, what if something happens to me?" That was when Poorna remembered her school's commandments. "The tenth commandment is 'I shall never give up' and that is my favourite," she says.

Minutes later, Poorna summited the mountain and hoisted our national flag. For Poorna, climbing Mount Everest proved "that girls can do anything".

Nandini Harinath, Minal Rohit and Seetha Somasundaram

SUPER SCIENTISTS

Nandini, Minal and Seetha held their breath as the Mars Orbiter Mission entered Mars's orbit. The mission was a success! Everyone at the Indian Space Research Organisation (ISRO) jumped from their seats in excitement; they could finally celebrate. The day was 24 September 2014 and the scientists had been working non-stop, often up to thirty-six hours at a time, just for this moment.

Nandini Harinath loved watching *Star Trek* as a young girl. But little did she know that one day her life would be more exciting than any film. She was responsible for 'inserting' the spacecraft into Mars's orbit – a very difficult task! "It was like hitting

the bullseye on a dartboard standing on the other side of the world," says Nandini.

For Minal Rohit, it was the sight of busy scientists wearing pristine white lab coats that first attracted her to science. She was the manager of the team that created important machines called payloads. These payloads would help detect the possibility of life on Mars and they had to be made within six months!

With limited time and a shoestring budget, the mission needed a leader who could guide the different teams. This was where Dr Seetha Somasundaram, the program director, stepped in. "She's a very strict lady." Minal laughs. But it was this strictness that helped Seetha guide the mission to success.

Today, thanks to the hard work of these super scientists, India has touched the stars, or should we say Mars. For them, even the sky is not the limit!

India is the first country to reach Mars in its first attempt.

INDEX

ACKNOWLEDGEMENTS

My first debt of gratitude is to my parents. Mom who told me so many of these stories in my childhood and who is still my favorite storyteller. Papa who, for months, sent me newsclips and articles about inspirational women to help with the research. You make the world go round.

To Darshan, my rock and my North Star. Thank you for always helping me find my course when I'm lost at sea, sometimes several times a day.

To Bagai, Kunty and Natasha who know that disappearances are temporary and that nothing else matters.

To Rinks Awtani, thank you for the love and your immense talent.

To Aditya 'Danny' Puar, thank you for being the first friend of this book and advocating for it as you did.

My gratitude to the brilliant team at Scholastic India is in order. To Sushmita, editor extraordinaire—thank you for making this book your own. You made a difficult process seem easy and for that I am forever grateful.

And finally to Shantanu, dear publisher, who believed in this book in an instant. Thank you for the pizza.

Neha J Hiranandani is a writer whose columns have appeared in *The Indian Express*, *Huffington Post*, NDTV and *Vogue* among others.

She holds degrees in Literature and Education from Wellesley College and Harvard University.